Salmon Patties &
Rosehip Pie Cookbook

ART, FOOD, AND THE COASTAL LIFE
IN HALIBUT COVE, ALASKA

Marian T. Beck
Recipes from the Saltry Restaurant

Marian T Beck

SALTRY PRESS™
HALIBUT COVE, ALASKA

To my husband, Dave, who throughout our life on the island together has helped me realize all my wild ideas, and to the community of Halibut Cove for all their support and laughter.

Copyright © 2011 by Marian T. Beck
Paintings and narrative captions copyright © by Marian T. Beck

Library of Congress Control Number: 2011926966
ISBN (HB): 978-0-615-47151-8

Published by Saltry Press™
P.O. Box 6410
Halibut Cove, Alaska 99603
www.thesaltry.com

First edition, 2004
Second edition, second printing 2012

Introduction by Kathleen Bennett
Project leader/production: Susan Dupèré
Managing editor: Kathy Howard
Designer: Brad Greene
Indexer: Cher Paul
Distribution: Epicenter Press/Aftershocks Media

Printed in China

Credits. All paintings by Marian T. Beck are alkyd oil on canvas. Front cover: *Rowboats*; Back cover: Dock at Halibut Cove (photo by Ted Bell); front flap: *Hand Purse Seining*; p.1: *Waiting for Snow*; p. 2: *Alaskan Wild Rose*; p. 6: *Lunch on the Sheep River* (© Pratt Museum PM.2007.21.1); p. 7: The *Danny J.* (photo by Ted Bell); p. 9: The *Saltry* on barge (photo by Dave Beck); p. 10: *The Tender Man*; p. 12: *Rusty's Lagoon*; p. 16: *Glacier*; p. 19: *Halibut Cove Sunrise*; p. 20: *Homer Fish Dock*; p. 23: *Coaling Skiff*; p. 26: *Fall Squall*; p. 29: *Outdated Outboards*; p. 30: *Night Clamming*; p. 33: *Double Hook-up*; p. 38: *Homer's Hay Fields*; p. 44: *Trolling for Kings*; p. 47: *Pulling in the Nets*; p. 50: *Hand Purse Seining*; p. 53: *Camp Cook*; p. 59: *Airstrip*; p. 60: *Natural Arch*; p. 64: *Listening to Silence*; p. 74: *Halibut Cove Style*; p. 77: *Kachemak Bay Homestead*; p. 86: *Waiting for Snow*; p. 89: *Rowboats*; p. 97: *Rosehips*; p. 100: *The Homer Hill*; p. 104: *Lagoon Fishing*; p. 106: *Island Ponies*; p. 107: Author and seal pup, Halibut Cove (photo collection of the author); p. 112: *An Adventure*; end sheets: *Out of the Fog*.

CONTENTS

INTRODUCTION

Halibut Cove 7

The Saltry 9

APPETIZERS

Saltry Bread 13

Salmon Pâté 14

Pickled Salmon 15

CEVICHE

Halibut Pickled with Citrus 17

Papaya Ceviche 18

POKE

Original Saltry Poke 21

Walter's Korean Poke 22

Vegetable Nori Rolls 24

Cinnamon Shrimp 25

Lucinda's Baked Oysters 27

Kachemak Bay Blue Mussels 28

SOUPS
& STEWS

Sable Fish Chowder 31

Fish Stock 32

Coconut Seafood Chowder 34

Trey's Bouillabaisse 35

Cioppino 36

Saltry Summer Soup 37

SALAD &
DRESSINGS

Vibrant Volcano Salad 39

Raspberry Poppy Seed Vinaigrette 40

Sweet Basil Dressing 41

Roasted Red Bell Pepper Dressing 41

Rhubarb and Bacon Vinaigrette 42

Refrigerator Pickles 43

HALIBUT

Grilled Halibut 45

Paprika Soy Halibut 45

Pesto Halibut 46

Halibut with Hot Bacon Dressing 48

Halibut Cakes with Garlic-Dill Aioli 48

SALMON

Sesame Ginger Salmon 51

Grilled Salmon with Raspberry Sauce 51

Dave's Salmon Patties 52

Stuffed China Poot Red 54

Smoked Salmon Yam Yums 55

Smoked Salmon Pasta 58

SHARK

Spicy Korean Shark with Papaya Salsa 61

Shark Pie 63

FAVORITE ENTRÉES

Marian's Buffalo Lasagna 65

Tony's Buffaloaf 67

Steven's Shrimp and Cod Lasagna 68

End of the Year Moose Ribs 71

Clay Duck 72

SIDE DISHES

Sesame Slaw 75

Sautéed Kale 75

Grilled Vegetables 76

Syd's Holualoa Coconut Rice 78

Shiitake Potato Cakes 79

Garlic Mashed Potatoes 80

Mushroom Ragout 81

Goat Cheese and Roasted Garlic Polenta 82

Blue Cheese Butter 83

Braised Fennel and Shiitake Mushrooms 84

Yellow Curry Sauce 85

DESSERTS

Swedish Crème 87

Crème Brûlée 88

Chocolate Cheesecake 90

Peanut Butter Pie 91

Alana's Kodiak Explosion Cake 92

Fig and Pecan Bread Pudding 94

Warm Soft Chocolate Cakes 95

Toby Tyler's Rosehip Pie 96

Toni's Cove-Style Apple Pie 98

Mom's Rhubarb Custard Pie 99

SMOKING
& SALTING
FISH

Smoking Fish 101

Smoking Marinade 102

Candied Salmon 102

Salting Fish 103

Acknowledgments 105

About the Artist 107

Index 109

Lunch on the Sheep River

Along the banks of the Sheep River, one of three that pour into Kachemak Bay, cattlemen gather to move the herds to and from the rich pastures of salt grass that fatten them from early spring and through the summer. However, there are times when the cattle become impatient and begin to head home to the farms on their own. Then, a hurriedly concocted group on horseback will gather at the cattlemen's cabin to drive them back across the river. The yellowing sunlight illuminating the blue glaciers and orange foliage of fall provides a spectacular setting for this adventure.

INTRODUCTION
Halibut Cove

The community of Halibut Cove, on the Kenai Peninsula, lies in a protected stretch of waterway called the narrows, which runs between hourglass-shaped Ismailof Island and the south shore of Kachemak Bay. Many of the houses sit on pilings, and the only transportation is by boat—there are no cars. The surrounding water of Kachemak Bay provides the livelihood of many residents. Local men and women fish commercially for salmon, halibut, or cod, and others maintain the three active oyster farms. There are also a number of artists in the Cove, and it's not unusual for a resident to be both artist and commercial fisher.

At present, about 30 people live in Halibut Cove full-time, with a summer population of almost 150. The boardwalk at Halibut Cove, although privately owned, has become a popular tourist destination, and each summer thousands of visitors

The ferry Danny J. *leaves Halibut Cove on its morning run to Homer.*

come to eat gourmet food at the Saltry, stroll the boardwalk, and enjoy the art galleries.

The landscape is dramatic. Mountains rise abruptly from the sea, and an expanse of water can be seen from any vantage. Shorebirds, seals, and otters swim up and down the narrows, and the endless days of summer cast a pink-hued light across the island.

The area is rich with history. Archaeological research of midden sites shows signs of a large settlement during prehistoric times. Artifacts found locally suggest three waves of native habitation, likely forced to leave because of a catastrophic event, such as a volcanic eruption.

From 1911 to 1928, a rich herring run in Halibut Cove led to a population boom. The herring fishery employed as many as 1,000 people during the height of the season. A town sprang up, and docks were built to accommodate the steamers that came to load kegs of salted fish. There was a pool hall, frequent dances, and, during Prohibition, a number of bootleggers.

By 1927, pollution from processing in the spawning grounds had caused a marked decline in the stocks, and by 1928 the herring were gone and the boom was over. Halibut Cove became a ghost town with only a few tenacious old-timers remaining. Buildings were torn down for material to build the growing village of Homer.

In 1948, Clem Tillion came to Halibut Cove. In 1952, he married Diana Rutzebeck, and they stayed to raise their children Will, Marian, Martha, and Vince. The Tillions helped foster the developing community. Clem started the ferry run to Homer in 1966, and Diana's Cove Gallery, featuring her paintings in octopus ink, opened in 1968. Their combined focus on business and art attracted a new generation of settlers. Halibut Cove began to rebuild.

The Saltry

O n an overcast day in the fall of 1983 the Saltry, jacked up and teetering on three-foot wooden stilts, floated slowly down the Halibut Cove channel, flanked by skiffs bearing "no wake" signs. Rising over all was the Saltry's steeply peaked and swooping roofline—attributes that had earlier caused the locals to dub it "the Flying Nun."

When the perfect building to house an island eatery presented itself, Marian and Dave Beck acted instantly to acquire the unique structure that became the Saltry Restaurant. A U-shaped dock was constructed in preparation for the Saltry's arrival. Moving day was chosen for its twenty-three-foot tide, the highest of the season. When the tide was at its highest point, the barge was eased into the U-shaped opening. As the tide dropped, the empty barge eased down and away with the tide. Pilings were erected from the beach at low tide to brace the Saltry from underneath. If you look at the dock around the Saltry now, it's possible to

The Saltry as a house-boat being moved to its new resting place on the dock.

The Tender Man

A fishing tender's job is to pick up the day's catch from the fishermen along the coast and take the fish to the buyer. Now and then, a shark will get caught in a set net. The tender calls the Saltry to send someone to pick it up and off they go in the Saltry skiff named The Skillet, bearing gifts of chocolate cheesecake for the tender and his sole crewmember, his daughter. The shark is destined for a plate of Spicy Korean Shark with Papaya Salsa or Shark Pie.

see how it sits not quite square, how its final settling place is slightly caddywhompus. The barge, in the nature of island things, has found another use and now houses fishermen's bunks, towed along to the fishing grounds in the summer salmon season. In the winter it lies tethered to a dock just down the channel.

The Saltry first opened its doors in April 1984. Eighty people arrived for the celebratory potluck, despite the howling blizzard of rain and snow. At its inception, the Saltry provided simple fare: drinks at a bar, hot chowder, fresh bread, and cold appetizers—such as pickled fish—that are still on the menu today. From these simple (and unusual) beginnings came a fair amount of press. Not long after its opening, *Alaska Magazine* featured a full-page spread on the Saltry. The article was seen by the producers of *Good Morning America,* prompting the filming of a vacation segment with Erma Bombeck, featuring the Saltry in Halibut Cove.

Marian and Dave remember the ash that covered everything after a volcanic eruption that March, and how they worked until the last minute in order to get everything clean before Ms. Bombeck, resplendent in fake pink fur, and her television crew arrived. The Saltry wasn't yet open for the season when the network came to film. The people eating, drinking beer, and playing the part of tourists in the video bear the familiar faces of the locals.

Today, the Saltry serves about 100 people every day of the summer season, dishing out gourmet food from a kitchen decidedly more sophisticated than in 1984. What hasn't changed is the incredibly beautiful setting of the Saltry, with its view of mountains and glaciers from its perch above the water.

This cookbook is intended to give a glimpse into the unique experience of life in an Alaskan island community through local recipes and the paintings of Marian Tillion Beck.

—Kathleen Bennett

Rusty's Lagoon

This lagoon was the home of a little freckle-faced man who set his traps in winter across the Grewingk Glacier flats. On the beach beyond the flats of the quiet lagoon, the pounding of ocean swells echoes their power and force. If he ever felt the need for social interaction, he could pick the day and row a couple of miles to Ismailof Island, where he had built another small cabin for summer use.

APPETIZERS

Saltry Bread

A Saltry original, with a sweet and nutty flavor.

2 tablespoons salt

6 cups whole wheat flour

6 cups white flour

1/8 cup yeast

4 cups warm water

1/2 cup honey

1/2 cup molasses

1/3 cup equal parts of millet,
   sesame seeds, and wheat bran

Preheat oven to 350°F.

Start with all ingredients at room temperature. Sift salt into the flour mixture. Dissolve the yeast into warm water, add honey, molasses, and 6 cups of flour. Mix in millet, sesame seeds, and wheat bran. Let rise until sponge has doubled its size. Mix in remaining 6 cups of flour, adding 1 at a time. Let the dough double in size, then knead heavily for at least 5 minutes. Shape into loaves. Bake at 350°F for 20 minutes, then lower temperature to 250°F and bake until brown.

VARIATION: For lighter bread, use 9 cups white flour and 3 cups wheat. Also, wheat bran may be substituted for 1/3 cup poppy seeds.

Serves 34

Salmon Pâté

1 medium red onion, halved

1 pound smoked salmon (see recipe page 102)

3 pounds cream cheese, softened at room temperature

1 cup sour cream

1 tablespoon paprika

1 teaspoon lemon juice

1 tablespoon tomato paste or juice

1 teaspoon hot chili sauce

3 scallions, chopped

Place half of red onion in food processor with 1 cup of smoked salmon. Salmon should be firm, not soft. Puree and set aside.

Beat cream cheese for 5 minutes, add sour cream, paprika, lemon juice, tomato paste or juice, hot chili sauce, and pureed onion and salmon; beat for 1 more minute. Dice remaining onion and salmon into small pieces. By hand, stir the scallions, the hand-chopped onion, and the smoked salmon into the mixture. The pâté should be stiff, not runny.

NOTE: This pâté makes a wonderful dish for a party. Serve with crackers or thinly sliced, toasted bread rounds. Garnish with chopped scallions or parsley and edible flowers, such as nasturtiums.

Serves 34

Pickled Salmon

    6 cups salted fish (see recipe page 103),
        cut into 1-inch cubes
    1 gallon white vinegar
   10 cups granulated sugar
    1 cup pickling spices
    8 cups sliced onion

Cover salted fish with ½ gallon white vinegar, and let sit for 24 hours. Dump vinegar off fish and dispose of it. Prepare a pickling bucket or covered container. Boil other ½ gallon of vinegar with sugar and spices. In bucket or container, stack fish in alternating layers with liberal amounts of onion. Pour brine over and keep refrigerated for 2 weeks before using.

Unlike the recipe on page 103, fish should be soaked in white vinegar, not water, to remove salt.

HINT: Pickled salmon in a glass jar makes a beautiful gift.

Serves 24

Glacier

Grewingk Glacier is in Halibut Cove's backyard. In the winter you can walk a mile and a half across the frozen lake, weaving between icebergs to stand at the glacier's base. After a warm spell, the ice is a deep aquamarine blue and the icebergs have melted into fantastical ice-castle shapes, laced with tunnels and topped with wavelike crests. The glacier is different at every visit, calving off in building-sized pieces and slowing retreating, leaving behind a barren landscape of deeply carved crevasses and ice-hewn rock.

Halibut Pickled with Citrus

2 large limes

2 large lemons

2 large oranges

3 tablespoons zest of lime, lemon, and orange

2 cubes chicken or vegetable bouillon,
    dissolved in 1/8 cup warm water

1 medium sweet red onion, diced

3 medium tomatoes, diced

2 teaspoons chili paste (more to taste)

1 cup de-stemmed and chopped cilantro

1/2 teaspoon cumin

4 cups halibut with skin removed,
    cut into bite-sized pieces

Grate the peels of limes, lemons, and oranges to get 3 tablespoons of zest, and toss into a large bowl or a plastic container. Squeeze the juice from all citrus, and add to zest. Add dissolved broth, onion, tomatoes, chili paste, cilantro, and cumin. Taste and adjust flavor as needed.

Add halibut; the juice should just cover the fish. If you need more juice, dissolve orange juice concentrate in water and add just until covered. Cover the bowl or container and refrigerate for at least 24 hours, allowing the citrus to "cook" the fish. (The smaller the pieces of fish, the less time it takes to cook.)

NOTE: Ceviche is a South American dish in which the fish is cooked by the acidity of the citrus juice. The other ingredients make up a type of salsa. There are no limitations on the type of

(continued)

seafood used, and we encourage you to experiment with the composition of the salsa. The Saltry crew complements this classic recipe with calamari, salad shrimp, and segments of grapefruit and orange.

Serves 12

Papaya Ceviche

   3 medium papayas, very ripe, cut into small chunks
   4 juicy limes (plus grated zest from the peel)
   1/2 cup tomato paste
   1 tablespoon finely minced ginger
   1 red pepper, chopped
   1 green pepper, chopped
   1 yellow pepper, chopped
   1 red onion, chopped
   1 cup cilantro, diced
   1 teaspoon cumin
   2 tablespoons roasted chili sauce
   3 tablespoons frozen orange juice dissolved
      in 1 cup water
   4 cups fresh halibut, skin removed and flesh cut
      into bite-sized pieces

Prepare the same as previous recipe.

HINT: Before juicing, place lemons and limes in a clean towel and roll vigorously either with your hands on a counter, or, for the adventurous cook, put them on the floor and roll them with your feet. This softens the fruit and makes them much easier to juice.

Serves 20

Halibut Cove Sunrise
with Purple Moon

Long summer days make for long workdays. In the early morning calm, the first out-board motor disturbs the quiet of the cove. There is great pleasure in checking and starting your boat, then untying it to set out on the daily adventure. There is no way to predict the day's weather. Tides and machinery rule the flow of activities. "You don't know till you go" is the motto Covers live by.

Homer Fish Dock

The Homer fish dock is lined with buyers surveying and purchasing a variety of fish from the daily selection. On this late July evening, three drift gillnetters are unloading their catch of salmon. These boats and crews had set out to sea at 2 A.M. the previous day to reach the fishing grounds thirty-five miles away. Fishing here in Cook Inlet is a game of hide-and-seek while fighting the weather, huge tides, and strong tidal rips. The prize in this game lies on display for the buyers on the dock.

POKE

There are as many types of poke as there are fish and ingredients. Poke is a Hawaiian dish not unlike the family stew—anything goes! At the Saltry we use hard salted salmon (see recipe page 103), but the possibilities are endless. Traditionally, poke is made with raw fish such as salmon, ahi, or shrimp. If you're tentative about the traditional version, we recommend you try cooked scallops, shrimp, halibut, ahi, or rockfish, or try lightly steamed clams or mussels.

Original Saltry Poke

1 tablespoon soy sauce

1 tablespoon rice wine vinegar

2 tablespoons sesame oil

1 teaspoon chili powder or chili sauce

2 teaspoons brown sugar

2 tablespoons pureed ginger

3 scallions, chopped, both green and white parts

1 tablespoon toasted sesame seeds

2 cups seafood of choice, cut into 1/4-inch cubes

Mix all ingredients except sesame seeds in a large bowl. Add seafood, cover bowl, and place in refrigerator for at least 2 hours, until the flavors absorb. Stir in sesame seeds.

Serves 8

Walter's Korean Poke

1/4 cup hot chili sauce

1 tablespoon pureed garlic

2 tablespoons pureed fresh ginger

1/2 medium red onion, minced or pureed

1/4 cup sesame oil

2 teaspoons hijiki seaweed (optional)

1 teaspoon sweet soy sauce

1 teaspoon soy sauce

3 cups seafood of choice, cut into bite-sized pieces

Chopped scallions (garnish)

Sesame seeds (garnish)

Mix all ingredients except scallions and sesame seeds together in a large bowl; toss with seafood of choice. Cover and let sit in refrigerator for at least 2 hours. Garnish and serve.

HINT: The spicy poke recipe is particularly wonderful when served with something cooling, such as ceviche.

VARIATION: For the fiery poke that Alaskans love, use Sriracha chili sauce and adjust the spice to taste. The Saltry serves this recipe with shrimp.

Serves 8

Coaling Skiff

It was a twelve-mile journey from Halibut Cove to the coaling beach. The day for gathering coal was chosen carefully. Piles of coal were staged between the skiff and the high tide line. As the tide came in, coal was loaded into the skiff. There was a balance in loading enough coal to make the trip worthwhile, but not overloading. Many a story can be told about coaling skiffs, bow-heavy with their load, being swamped just moments from home.

Vegetable Nori Rolls

2 cups sushi rice

2 eggs

1 tablespoon granulated sugar

2 tablespoons sesame oil

1 tablespoon rice wine vinegar

1 large carrot, peeled and cut into slivers

1 small cucumber, seeded and cut into slivers

1 avocado, cut into slivers

Toasted sesame seeds

4 sheets nori

Put the rice on to cook; the usual ratio for sushi rice is 1 cup rice per $1^1/2$ cups water. As it cooks, prepare the filling. Beat the eggs in a small bowl with the sugar. Coat a hot fry pan with sesame oil, then add egg. Allow to brown on bottom side, using a spatula to keep egg from sticking. Flip, trying to keep it in 1 piece, like a pancake. When egg is cooked, turn out on cutting board to cool.

When rice is finished, stir in rice vinegar while fanning the rice with your other hand. Do this fanning/stirring routine for at least a minute, or until the rice is sticky enough to form into balls and cool enough to handle.

Set up a work station: Set all vegetables, sesame seeds, egg (sliced about 1 inch wide), rice, and a bowl of water around a cutting board. Place a sheet of nori, short side facing you, on the board. Using your hands, put about $1/2$ cup of rice on nori and push around (wetting your hands with the water helps) until nori is covered except for $1^1/2$ or 2 inches at the top. $1^1/2$ inches from the bottom, place the vegetables and egg horizontally. Sprinkle with sesame seeds then roll up, wetting the rice-less strip at the top with water to close. Slice into rounds using a sharp knife wiped with a damp cloth between each slice. Serve with wasabi, soy sauce, and pickled ginger.

Serves 12

Cinnamon Shrimp

1 cup cinnamon
3 cups light oil
1 pound large shrimp, shelled but with tails
Salt to taste
Chili paste (optional)

Make cinnamon oil by placing cinnamon in fine sieve (a coffee filter in a cone works fine.) Slowly pour oil through. This will make about $2^{1}/_{2}$ cups of cinnamon oil. Put oil in an empty gallon jar with shrimp and refrigerate for at least 2 hours, shaking occasionally. If desired, add salt and chili paste to oil and shake vigorously to mix. Either grill the shrimp on skewers with vegetables such as zucchini, tomatoes, and mushrooms, or brown in cinnamon oil on the stove.

Makes 12 skewers

Fall Squall

In the late summer, the weather on Kachemak Bay can become quite frisky. Blown in with the whipping winds are the silver salmon called coho. Sarah Baxter, who sets her nets on McDonald Spit, is usually the last to give up her quest because of the weather. One blustery day when the Saltry needed fish, Marian guided her skiff four-teen miles down the coast to see what she could get from Sarah. As the set net and its proprietor came into view from the small boat, and the sea had already risen into frothy peaks from the howling wind, there was Sarah stubbornly picking her net, just as she had done for more than forty years.

Lucinda's Baked Oysters

A recipe straight from the oyster farmer.

24 good-sized oysters

2 to 3 cups rock salt
(enough for bottom of a baking pan)

1½ cylinders Club butter crackers
(Lucinda says not to substitute other kinds)

5 cloves garlic, minced

½ pound clarified butter

Salt and pepper to taste

Chopped parsley (optional, for garnish)

Preheat oven to 450°F.

Open oysters, being careful not to get shell fragments on the meat. Throw away top of shell but leave oyster in the bottom half. Drain off half of liquid (you can save this for other recipes such as chowder). Cut the muscle at the bottom of the shell away from the meat. Fill baking pan with rock salt and nestle in the oysters so that they don't tip.

Run crackers through a food processor, and place in a bowl. Sautée the garlic in clarified butter and add to the crackers. Place a spoonful of cracker mixture on each oyster. Place in oven for about 6 minutes, or until golden brown. Garnish with chopped parsley (if using), season with salt and pepper, and serve.

HINT: Fill the bottom of the serving dish with rock salt to make an attractive presentation that will prevent the oysters from tipping.

Serves 12

Kachemak Bay Blue Mussels

A delicious and simple way to enjoy fresh mussels.

2 pounds mussels, cleaned
(approximately 1/2 pound mussels per person)

5 tablespoons butter

2 tablespoons minced garlic

2 cups white wine

Place all ingredients into a deep frying pan on medium-high heat. Cover with a tight lid. Allow to cook until mussels open, about 5 minutes. Keep an eye on the liquid while cooking; you may need to add 1/2 cup more wine. Keep in mind that all ingredient amounts must be adjusted according to the amount of mussels. These amounts are for about 2 pounds of mussels.

HINT: Try serving this as a main course with a salad and fresh bread for dipping in the broth. Adjust the mussel amount to 1 pound per serving.

Serves 2 to 4

Outdated Outboards

Nothing ever gets thrown away on this island. Everything is carefully saved with the idea that some part of it will probably be needed some day. Outdated outboards, no longer running and hardly repairable, are still too good to discard.

Night Clamming

In the winter, minus tides occur at night and clamming must be done in the dark. Marian remembers cold and clear nights, walking down the beach with her whole family, the glow from a kerosene lantern fading out across the muddy shore.

Sable Fish Chowder

A substantial chowder with a wonderful, smoky taste.

2 tablespoons garlic

2 tablespoons butter

2 cups fresh mushrooms

1/2 cup white wine

3 strips bacon, chopped

1 cup chopped onions

2 cups chopped carrots

2 cups chopped celery

2 teaspoons fresh rosemary

2 teaspoons thyme

2 cups potatoes, peeled and cut into bite-sized pieces

2 quarts clam juice

2 cups chopped clams

2 cups smoked sable fish (see recipe page 102)

1 cup evaporated milk or cream

This chowder is best made in parts and assembled just before serving.

In a small pan, brown garlic in butter. Add mushrooms, then wine. Cook off wine and set aside. In a soup pot, cook bacon until firm. It should not be crispy. Add onions, cooking until translucent. Add carrots, celery, herbs, and potatoes. Cook until

(continued)

carrots are nearly soft. Add clam juice and gently boil. When vegetables are tender, stir in the chopped clams.

Before serving, add 2 tablespoons smoked sable fish and evaporated milk or cream to each bowl, then pour your soup over it. Top with a spoonful of mushrooms.

NOTE: For a richer base, use heavy cream. The sautéed mushrooms are optional.

Serves 24

Fish Stock

Olive oil for pot

2 onions, chopped

4 cloves garlic, minced

2 carrots, chopped

4 stalks celery, leaves and all

Bay leaf

1 teaspoon marjoram

1/2 teaspoon rosemary

1 teaspoon dill

About 3 pounds fish parts
   (bones, heads, shrimp husks, etc.)

1 cup white wine

1/2 teaspoon pepper

Salt to taste

In a large pot coated with oil, sauté onions, garlic, carrots, celery, and herbs. When garlic and onions are brown, add everything else. Bring to a boil then simmer for 1 to 2 hours.

Double Hook-up

Winter fishing is done by trolling off shore in deep water. Today the falling snow gives a wonderful sense of aloneness and quiet, as though the fighting fish and the fisherman are the only things on earth. It is not unusual to run into a little school of feeder king salmon; they are cruising around the North Pacific gaining fat for the inevitable task of swimming upriver to spawn.

Coconut Seafood Chowder

1 clove garlic, minced

1 leek, chopped

1 tablespoon chopped fresh ginger

1 small red onion, diced

4 tablespoons butter

4 carrots, sliced in rounds

1/2 cup chopped celery

1/2 cup chopped red pepper

1 (13-ounce) can baby corn

2 1/2 cups milk

2 (13-ounce) cans coconut milk

3 tablespoons hot chili sauce

1 stalk lemongrass

2 cups salmon, cut into bite-sized pieces

2 cups halibut, cut into bite-sized pieces

1 pound clams in shell

2 tablespoons finely chopped basil

2 tablespoons finely chopped cilantro

In a medium-sized pot, sauté the garlic, leek, ginger, and onion in butter. Add carrots, celery, red pepper, and baby corn. Stir for 2 minutes. Add milk, coconut milk, and chili sauce. Toss in lemongrass stalk. Add clams and fish and cook on medium heat until clams are open and fish is cooked. Garnish with basil and cilantro. Serve.

NOTE: Experiment with the type of seafood you use. Try shrimp and mussels and scallops.

Serves 12

Trey's Bouillabaisse

1/3 cup diced onion

2 cloves garlic, minced

Olive oil for the soup pot

1 tablespoon paprika

2 (15-ounce) cans stewed tomatoes

1 (8-ounce) can tomato sauce

1 cup fish stock

12 ounces fresh fish (halibut, salmon, rock fish, etc.)

12 ounces clams, steamed then chopped

8 ounces mussels

8 ounces large shrimp

1/4 cup finely chopped parsley

1/4 cup finely chopped basil

Salt and pepper to taste

In a soup pot, sauté onion and garlic over low heat. When onions are translucent, add paprika and stir. Add stewed tomatoes, tomato sauce, and fish stock. Heat slowly and add fish, clams, mussels, and shrimp. When mussel shells are open, add parsley and basil, salt and pepper. Simmer until fish is cooked.

Serves 12

Cioppino

A spicy Italian seafood stew.

1/8 cup olive oil

2 tablespoons butter

1 large white onion, peeled and finely chopped

2 cloves garlic, minced

1 medium carrot, finely chopped

1/2 medium green pepper, chopped

1/2 medium red pepper, chopped

1 small leek, finely chopped (white part only)

1 small stalk celery, chopped

2 (28-ounce) cans diced tomatoes, including liquid

8 ounces dry white wine

1/8 cup honey

1 tablespoon chopped fennel

1 tablespoon basil (1/4 cup if fresh)

1 tablespoon oregano (1/4 cup if fresh)

1 teaspoon thyme (1 tablespoon if fresh)

4 bay leaves

1 pound clams

1 pound mussels, de-bearded and cleaned

1 pound halibut, cut into bite-sized pieces

Dash cayenne pepper

Salt and black pepper to taste

In a large pot, heat oil and butter, and add onion, garlic, carrot, peppers, leek, and celery. Sauté until soft. Add tomatoes, wine, honey, fennel, and herbs. Simmer for 1 hour. Add clams, mussels, and fish, simmer an additional 10 to 15 minutes or until fish flakes when prodded with a fork, and mussels and clams open.

Add cayenne pepper and season with salt and pepper. Be careful not to overcook.

Serves 12

Saltry Summer Soup

3 cups water

3 cups chicken stock

1 small ginger root, sliced

3/4 cup fresh or frozen peas

3/4 cup slivered carrots

1/2 cup slivered red pepper

1 cup corn

1/2 cup chopped scallions

Cilantro, chopped (garnish)

Peanuts, chopped (garnish)

In a soup pot, bring water and chicken stock to a boil. Add all ingredients except cilantro and peanuts. Simmer for 10 minutes. Garnish and serve.

Serves 12

Homer's Hay Fields

A view from the hay fields on the north shore of Kachemak Bay reveals the glaciers, craggy cliffs, and surf-torn beaches of the south shore-line. July is harvest time on both the farms of the north shore and for the frenzied fishing boats in the waters off the south shore. Each pro-vides the necessities of life for the inhabitants of this soon to be snow-bound land.

SALAD & DRESSINGS

Fresh seafood atop garden greens is popular lunch fare at the Saltry and is often served alongside our classic homemade chowder or soup of the day. We offer a choice of grilled local fish: halibut, salmon, scallops, shrimp, or salmon shark, as availability allows.

Vibrant Volcano Salad

1 bag spring mix greens

3 carrots, julienned

1 cup thinly sliced purple cabbage

1 small can baby corn

1 tomato, cut into wedges

1 sliced beet, raw or boiled

1 medium red bell pepper, sliced into rings

1 medium cucumber, cut into thin, round slices

2 cups cooked seafood of choice

Fresh, colorful ingredients are key to this salad. Arrange the lettuce loosely in a salad bowl, making a small depression in the middle. Use the depression to prop up the carrots vertically in the bowl. They should seek impressive height. Arrange the remaining ingredients in the manner that best tickles your senses. Top with your favorite Saltry dressing.

NOTE: For best results slice cabbage thinly using a mandoline; carrots are also best prepared with a mandoline. When done

(continued)

properly, salad should have height and be bursting with both color and flavor. Feel free to get creative with garnish: A salad can be as artful as its maker!

CARAMELIZED PECANS

1/2 cup pecans
1/4 cup honey
Pinch salt

Heat honey and salt in pan. Add pecans and toss.

MENU SUGGESTION: Top with caramelized pecans and serve with Saltry Summer Soup (see recipe page 37) and fresh bread. Finish with Chocolate Cheesecake (see recipe page 90).

Serves 12

Raspberry Poppy Seed Vinaigrette

4 cups frozen raspberries
1 cup white distilled vinegar
1 1/2 cups canola oil
3 tablespoons Dijon mustard
1/2 cup poppy seeds
1/2 cup orange juice concentrate
2 teaspoons honey
Salt and pepper to taste

Blend all ingredients in blender until frothy.

NOTE: The Basil and Raspberry dressings are excellent served as a duo.

Makes 2 quarts

Sweet Basil Dressing

1 cup rice wine vinegar

1 1/2 cups canola oil

1/2 cup fresh basil

2 teaspoons honey

1/2 teaspoon chopped garlic

Salt and pepper to taste

Place all ingredients in a blender and blend until frothy.

Makes 3 cups

Roasted Red Bell Pepper Dressing

4 cups roasted red bell peppers

1 cup white distilled vinegar

1 1/2 cups canola oil

2 tablespoons Dijon mustard

1/2 cup orange juice concentrate

2 teaspoons honey

Salt and pepper to taste

Blend all ingredients in blender until frothy.

MENU SUGGESTION: This dressing is excellent over a salad with goat cheese and grilled halibut. Candied pecans complete the combination to make our most popular salad entrée.

Makes 2 quarts

Rhubarb and Bacon Vinaigrette

4 slices thick-cut bacon

1 shallot, minced

1/2 cup balsamic vinegar

1 tablespoon Dijon or whole grain mustard

2 tablespoons olive oil

1/2 teaspoon kosher salt

1/2 teaspoon ground black pepper

1 cup diced rhubarb

In a sauté pan, cook bacon over medium heat until crispy. Remove bacon, chop fine, and set aside. Leave the leftover grease in the pan. Add shallot and sauté for 1 minute. Add balsamic vinegar and reduce by a quarter. Whisk in mustard, olive oil, salt, and pepper. Add rhubarb and turn off heat. Serve over seared scallops, sablefish, or halibut. Garnish with reserved bacon bits.

Salad for 12

Refrigerator Pickles

6 medium pickling cucumbers

Kosher salt

1 teaspoon yellow mustard seeds

1 teaspoon cumin seeds

1 teaspoon coriander seeds

1 teaspoon black peppercorns

1 tablespoon curry powder

3 whole garlic cloves

1 small ginger bulb, thinly sliced

2 thick slices yellow onion

1 jalapeño, cut lengthwise

2 cups apple cider vinegar

2 cups water

2 tablespoons kosher salt

5 tablespoons sugar

1/2 cup chopped fresh dill

Slice cucumbers into 1/2-inch-thick half moons. Toss slices with a fair amount of kosher salt in a medium-sized bowl and let stand for 1/2 hour. Drain in a colander. In a small sauce pan, heat and stir mustard seeds, cumin, coriander, and peppercorns until fragrant. Turn off heat and add remaining ingredients except dill. Bring to a boil and let steep while cucumbers are draining. Rinse cucumbers and place into large jar or plastic container. Cover with pickling liquid, add dill, and refrigerate overnight. Pickles will keep for 2 weeks.

Serves 12

Trolling for Kings

Halibut Cove's palette is ever-shifting. The early mornings of late summer and early fall are blue. The cliffs of Peterson Point cast a deep shadow, forming a lane in which trolling boats travel.

HALIBUT

At the Saltry, almost all of our fish is served grilled. Some of our most popular recipes feature fresh fish grilled outside and served with a simple sauce. Here is a basic method for grilling halibut and a few recipes to try.

Grilled Halibut

To grill halibut effectively steaks must be substantial, but not more than 1½ inches thick.

Preheat the grill and oil it. Oil the fish and rub it with a mixture of salt and pepper. If fish has skin on it, begin with that side facing up. A general rule for grilling fish is 10 minutes per inch of thickness, so about 5 minutes each side. Still, be sure to check the fish carefully to make sure it's done—it should be opaque and quite firm.

Paprika Soy Halibut

1 cup soy sauce

1 tablespoon paprika

1 tablespoon brown sugar

2 cloves garlic, minced

4 to 12 halibut steaks

Make a marinade of soy sauce, paprika, sugar, and garlic. Marinate halibut in the refrigerator for at least 2 hours (make sure to turn it over). Grill according to directions above.

Enough sauce for 4 to 12 servings

Pesto Halibut

4 cups fresh basil leaves

5 cloves of garlic, peeled

1/2 cup pecans

3/4 cup olive oil

Salt and pepper to taste

3/4 cup grated Parmesan cheese

4 to 12 halibut steaks, grilled

Place all ingredients except fish and cheese in a food processor and blend until smooth. Stir in the cheese by hand. Warm the pesto and place on top of grilled halibut for an incredible and fresh-tasting dish.

NOTE: For local flare, the Saltry adds 2 cups of nasturtium leaves to the recipe.

Enough pesto for 4 to 12 servings

Pulling In the Nets

Boats using drift gillnets fish for salmon and look for their best catches in the tidal currents called "tidal rips." One side of the rip sucks the net in, and the other side spits it out. In-between is anything but calm. In Cook Inlet, the tides can reach up to thirty-three feet, and if combined with cold, wet, and rough weather from the Gulf of Alaska. Fish hit the nets hard in sloppy weather, keeping everyone's spirits high.

Halibut
with Hot Bacon Dressing

12 slices bacon, cooked and minced

1/2 cup balsamic vinegar

Black pepper

4 halibut steaks, grilled

Cook minced bacon in small pan with vinegar and pepper until liquid is reduced and dressing is stiff. Spoon on top of grilled halibut and serve with Garlic Mashed Potatoes (see recipe page 80) and Grilled Vegetables (see recipe page 76).

Serves 4

Halibut Cakes
with Garlic-Dill Aioli

AIOLI

2 egg yolks

6 cloves garlic, peeled

2 teaspoons Dijon mustard

1 teaspoon pepper

Pinch of salt

2 tablespoons lemon juice

2 tablespoons fresh dill

1 cup olive oil

Combine egg yolks, garlic, mustard, salt, pepper, lemon juice, and dill in a food processor. With the machine still on, slowly add olive oil until the mixture is thick and smooth. Keep refrigerated.

CAKES

½ pound halibut

1½ pounds halibut, cut into bite-sized chunks

½ cup bread crumbs

1 egg

¼ cup scallions

¼ red pepper, chopped

2 tablespoons parsley

1 tablespoon lemon juice

1 tablespoon fresh orange zest

½ red onion, chopped

1 teaspoon crushed garlic

Blend ½ pound of halibut in a food processor. In a large bowl, mix processed halibut, bread crumbs, egg, scallions, red pepper, parsley, lemon juice, zest, onion, and garlic. Add 1½ pounds of halibut chunks. Form into 10 patties. Fry in butter until golden brown.

MENU SUGGESTION: Halibut cakes and aioli go beautifully with Garlic Mashed Potatoes (see recipe page 80) and Sautéed Kale (see recipe page 75).

NOTE: This recipe is equally good with salmon. Halibut and salmon cakes served alongside one another are quite a treat.

Enough aioli for 12 cakes or 24 appetizer size

Hand Purse Seining

Marian and brothers Will and Vince are hauling in the "money bag" after circling fish in shallow waters with a net and chasing them into it with plungers. About 4,000 fish were caught per set, and at the end of each day they would throw the fish up to the waiting tender. Skewering the fish on poles to throw them, Marian remembers, her big brother Will could get as many as nine humpies on at once. They slept in a fishing shack perched on a scow, subsisting on Spam and canned corned beef and developing a taste for cowboy coffee, in which grounds were added every day, but never taken out. Marian saved her money from that fishing trip and bought her first saddle, a fancy western one with all the trimmings.

SALMON

Salmon is a wonderfully rich and versatile fish. We use only wild salmon, not farmed. It is much better tasting and much better for you.

Sesame Ginger Salmon

3/4 cup soy sauce

1/4 cup sesame oil

1/4 cup brown sugar

2 tablespoons minced garlic

2 tablespoons grated fresh ginger

1 tablespoon roasted chili paste

4 to 12 salmon fillets

Whisk together all ingredients except salmon, making sure to dissolve sugar. Marinate salmon in refrigerator for at least 6 hours, turning occasionally. Grill.

MENU SUGGESTION: Try serving with Syd's Coconut Rice (see recipe page 78) and Grilled Vegetables (see recipe page 76).

Enough sauce for 4 to 12 servings

Grilled Salmon with Raspberry Sauce

2 tablespoons butter

1 cup raspberries, fresh or frozen

1/4 cup balsamic vinegar

2 pinches white pepper

4 to 12 salmon fillets

(continued)

In a small saucepan, heat butter. Add raspberries, balsamic vinegar, and white pepper; reduce. If you prefer not to have seeds, strain through a fine sieve or cheesecloth. Serve over grilled salmon fillets.

Enough sauce for 4 to 12 servings

Dave's Salmon Patties

1 pound canned salmon or fresh fillets,
    put through a food processor

1 cup diced onion

2 large eggs

1½ cups cracker or bread crumbs

Oil or butter for pan

Mix all ingredients together and shape into patties. Fry until golden brown on both sides. For the traditional version, fry in bear fat instead of oil.

MENU SUGGESTION: Serve with Rosehip Pie (see recipe page 96), of course!

Serves 4

Camp Cook

Camping is all about the fire pit and preparing food—and poking the fire. You can make China Poot Red in a camp fire pit wrapped in alder leaves and covered with hot rocks. Food always tastes better around a campfire.

Stuffed China Poot Red

China Poot red salmon would be the local choice for this recipe, but any wild salmon will do.

4 to 6 pounds wild salmon, whole with bones removed

2 cups cooked rice (brown or wild)

2 cups mushrooms

1 medium red onion, finely chopped

2 tablespoons minced garlic

2 tablespoons butter

1/2 cup white wine

1 cup sour cream

1 cup chopped crab

1/4 cup chopped fresh basil

Salt and pepper to taste

Alder leaves (optional)

Preheat oven to 350°F.

Gut and gill fish. Remove bones by sliding a knife along the backbone, separating flesh from bone. Flip fish over and repeat. Be careful not to puncture the skin. Brown the garlic in the butter. Add mushrooms and cook for 2 minutes. Add wine and cook until most of the liquid has evaporated. Cool. Mix together rice, mushrooms, onion, sour cream, crab, and basil, then add salt and pepper to taste. Stuff fish, then sew fish belly shut with a carpet needle and beading twine, or use a metal skewer (sharp enough to pierce fish skin) and weave it in and out to seal the stuffing in.

For best flavor wrap fish in foil lined with alder leaves. Bake slowly for about an hour or until internal temperature of fish is 280°F.

NOTE: This is a fun meal to cook in an outdoor fire pit. Adjust cooking time to approximately 2 hours, (this depends on the size and heat of your fire) and check fish carefully to make sure it's done. Serve with other fire pit goodies, such as foil-wrapped potatoes and corn on the cob.

Serves 12

Smoked Salmon Yam Yums

1 red bell pepper

1 yellow bell pepper

1 tablespoon olive oil

1/2 cup sliced mushrooms

1/2 red onion

2 teaspoons garlic

2 yams, baked and skinned

2 pounds smoked salmon (see recipe page 102)

1 batch Saltry Bread dough, unbaked (see recipe page 13)

Salt and pepper to taste

1 egg

1/2 cup water

16 ounces grated Havarti cheese

(continued)

Preheat oven to 375°F.

Roast the bell peppers and cut into 1/4-inch strips. Heat the olive oil in a medium saucepan. Sauté mushrooms, onion, and garlic until browned. Drain excess oil and toss in peppers. Slice the yams and break up smoked salmon to be layered.

To prepare bread pockets, roll dough into thin oval shapes. They should be about 8 inches by 5 inches. On one half of the oval, layer the yam, salmon, sautéed vegetables, and cheese evenly. Sprinkle with salt and pepper. Fold the other half of the oval over and go around the edges with a fork, pressing the sides closed. The pouches should be full, so don't skimp when layering. Beat the egg and water together. Place the pockets on a baking sheet lined with parchment. Paint with egg wash and let sit out for about 30 minutes to allow the bread to rise. Bake for 25 minutes or until golden brown. Remaining dough could be used to make a loaf of bread, rolls, or cinnamon rolls.

HINT: Great for the saddlebag or over a campfire at the edge of the glacier.

Serves 24

Octopus Hunter

To catch an octopus is very hard. You must tread as lightly as a cat and you must never let your shadow cross their door, or they will hide until the tide comes in, then slip away. Their dens are made under rocks, and their living space is a puddle of water. They lie in their puddle and eat clams and crab and throw the empty shells out the door—a telltale sign they live there. They are very smart and have the keen eyesight of a dog—it's a rare hunter who is wilier than the octopus.

Smoked Salmon Pasta

1 teaspoon minced garlic

1/4 cup butter

1/4 cup vodka

1/2 cup heavy cream

3/4 cup shredded smoked salmon (see recipe page 102)

1/2 cup fresh peas

1 pound penne or fettucine

1/2 cup grated Parmesan cheese

1/4 cup sliced basil

Sauté garlic in butter. Add vodka and reduce. Add heavy cream and reduce. Add salmon and peas; cook for a few more minutes. Pour sauce over cooked pasta and garnish with Parmesan and basil.

Serves 4 to 6

Airstrip

Sometimes names are the last reminder of the past. The airstrip today is a pasture fading into an alder tunnel. It would take a vivid imagination to think of landing planes there.

Natural Arch

The natural arch marks the entrance to the protected waters of Halibut Cove. At high tide kayakers can paddle through the hole in the rock. At low tide beach walkers can discover a wide assortment of sea plants and creatures.

SHARK

Salmon shark are occasionally brought into the Saltry as the bycatch of the salmon fishery. The meat is white and dense, not unlike pork, and is a wonderful treat.

Spicy Korean Shark with Papaya Salsa

SHARK

4 cloves garlic, peeled

1 medium red onion, chopped

1 cup soy sauce

1/4 cup sweet soy sauce

1/4 cup balsamic vinegar

2 tablespoons roasted chili sauce

1/2 cup brown sugar

3 tablespoons grated fresh ginger

1/4 cup sesame oil

4 to 12 salmon shark steaks

Puree the garlic and onion in a food processor. Add all ingredients except for the shark and blend for a minute more. Pour into baking pan and add shark. Marinate, covered and refrigerated, for at least 4 hours. Grill for approximately 6 minutes each side—remember that the rule of thumb for cooking fish is 10 minutes for each inch of thickness—adjust cooking time accordingly. The meat will be white and flaky and similar to pork when finished.

(continued)

SALSA

4 juicy limes

6 medium papayas, very ripe, cut into small chunks

1/2 cup tomato paste

1 tablespoon finely minced ginger

1 red pepper, finely chopped

1 green pepper, finely chopped

1 yellow pepper, finely chopped

1 red onion, diced

1 cup chopped cilantro leaves

1 teaspoon cumin

2 tablespoons roasted chili sauce

Squeeze limes and put juice and all other ingredients in a bowl. Flavor will be best if the salsa sits for at least 2 hours.

Enough salsa for 4 to 12 servings

Shark Pie

2¹/₂ tablespoons rice wine vinegar

2 tablespoons yellow miso paste

¹/₄ cup olive oil

1 tablespoon sesame oil

1 teaspoon soy sauce

1 teaspoon chili paste

4 cups cooked Korean shark, cut into small pieces

2 cups mixed salad greens

3 tablespoons sesame seeds

1 (9-inch) pie shell, prebaked

In a small bowl, mix vinegar, miso, olive and sesame oils, soy sauce, and chili paste. Whisk vigorously to dissolve miso. In a large bowl, combine shark, greens, and sesame seeds. Toss with vinaigrette and put in pie shell. Serve.

Serves 12

Listening to Silence

Rural Alaskans take the autumn of each year very seriously. It is harvest time and time for adventure, as well. Progress is slowed and restaurants close—it is moose season and time for the hunt. Horses, fat on salt grass, relax on a windless day. Now at rest in their silent pasture, they will soon be back to work packing the moose meat out from the remote hunting camps.

Marian's Buffalo Lasagna

1 cup diced parsley, divided

1 cup sliced mushrooms

1 sliced tomato

1 cup diced green pepper

1 cup diced celery

1 cup diced onion

1 cup diced mushrooms

3 cups cubed tomatoes

2 tablespoons diced garlic

3 cups chopped fresh basil

1/2 teaspoon each thyme, marjoram,
  and oregano

6 ounces tomato paste

15 ounces tomato sauce

2 1/2 pounds ground buffalo

Salt and pepper to taste

3 tablespoons chili sauce

1 package lasagna noodles

32 ounces sour cream

32 ounces cottage cheese

Olive oil for greasing the pan

3/4 pound sharp Cheddar cheese, grated
  or sliced for topping

(continued)

Set aside ¼ cup parsley, the sliced mushrooms, and sliced tomato. Sauté the remaining vegetables and spices in olive oil. Add tomato paste and tomato sauce; simmer. In a separate pan, lightly brown the buffalo over medium-high heat with olive oil. Use just enough oil to keep it from sticking. Season with salt and pepper. Add chili sauce to taste; 4 tablespoons is the locals' favorite. Add buffalo to the vegetable mixture and continue simmering.

Boil noodles with a pinch of salt until al dente. In a medium bowl, mix sour cream and cottage cheese together. Coat a large baking pan (13 by 10 by 2½-inch) with olive oil and begin layering components as follows: noodles, meat and vegetables, then sour cream and cottage cheese. Continue until pan is full. Some noodles may be left over. Spread the mushrooms, parsley, and sliced tomato that were set aside earlier over the top, along with the Cheddar cheese. Preheat oven to 350°F. Cover with tin foil and bake for 30 minutes. Remove the foil and brown topping at 375°F for 15 minutes.

MENU SUGGESTION: Serve with grilled asparagus and a Mediterranean salad for a full-bodied meal.

COMPANION SALAD

2 large heads of romaine lettuce, torn

½ cup crumbled feta cheese

½ cup kalamata olives

DRESSING

1 tablespoon crushed garlic

½ cup balsamic vinegar

½ cup olive oil

Serves 14

Tony's Buffaloaf

1 large carrot

1 stalk celery

1/2 cup mushrooms

1 small bell pepper

1/2 medium-sized zucchini

1/2 medium-sized red onion

1 teaspoon garlic

1 teaspoon Dijon mustard

1/2 teaspoon salt

1/2 teaspoon pepper

3 eggs

1 1/2 cups bread crumbs

2 pounds ground buffalo

Cut vegetables into 1/2-inch pieces and put into food processor with garlic. Blend until no large bits are left. Set aside. Mix mustard, salt, pepper, and eggs thoroughly. In a large bowl, combine vegetables, spices, bread crumbs, and buffalo. Work together with hands until the texture is consistent. Form evenly into a log shape in a shallow baking pan. Be careful not to compress the mixture. Leaving the loaf fluffy creates juicy pockets and makes for a moist product.

LOAF COAT

1/2 cup ketchup

3 tablespoons molasses

1 teaspoon red chili sauce

1/2 teaspoon crushed garlic

Whisk all ingredients together.

(continued)

Preheat oven to 375°F.

Generously spread loaf coat over uncooked loaf. Bake for 1/2 hour. Be careful not to overbake. Prepare loaf sauce while you wait.

LOAF SAUCE

1 cup ketchup

3 tablespoons molasses

2 tablespoons hot chili sauce (Sriracha or Sambal)

Whisk together and drizzle over loaf before serving. Enjoy!

MENU SUGGESTION: Serve with Garlic Mashed Potatoes (see recipe page 80) and Grilled Vegetables (see recipe page 76) to tap into the local's favorite Saltry meal.

Serves 14

Steven's Shrimp and Cod Lasagna

SAUCE

1/2 cup butter

1 cup flour

2 tablespoons paprika

1/2 cup white wine

1 tablespoon fish sauce

1 tablespoon soy sauce

1 1/2 quarts fish or shrimp stock

1 cup heavy cream

1 cup milk

1 teaspoon salt

Juice from 1/2 lemon

In a medium saucepan, melt butter and cook until it no longer foams. Whisk in flour and paprika. Cook, stirring, for 2 minutes. Whisk in remaining sauce ingredients, except for lemon juice. Bring to a boil and reduce heat. Simmer for 15 minutes. Remove from heat and add lemon juice.

FILLING

1 pound softened cream cheese

1 pound goat cheese

2 tablespoons chopped fresh tarragon

2 tablespoons chopped flat-leaf parsley

Zest from 1 lemon

Juice from $1/2$ lemon

1 teaspoon salt

1 teaspoon freshly ground pepper

Combine all ingredients thoroughly.

FRESH COMPONENTS

8 ounces shiitake mushrooms, sliced

1 medium zucchini, sliced in half moons

1 large red pepper, julienned

1 small yellow onion, julienned

1 pound cod, cut into $1/2$-inch cubes

1 pound cooked shrimp

1 package lasagna noodles

Salt and pepper to taste

Freshly grated Parmesan cheese

(continued)

ASSEMBLY

Preheat oven to 350ºF.

Use a 9-by-13-inch baking dish. From bottom to top, layer the ingredients as follows: 1 cup sauce, 1 layer of uncooked noodles, $1/2$ of the cream cheese mixture spread evenly, and all of the mushrooms, zucchini, and cod. Then comes the next layer: 1 cup sauce, 1 layer of uncooked noodles, the remaining cream cheese mixture spread evenly, and all of the red pepper, onion, and shrimp. For the final layer, use 1 cup sauce, a layer of uncooked noodles, and cover with sauce.

Cover baking dish with parchment paper and then foil and bake for 1 hour. When done, you should be able to easily insert a knife into the noodles. Uncover and generously cover with Parmesan cheese. Return to oven for 15 minutes. Let lasagna rest for $1/2$ hour. Not doing so will result in loose and messy lasagna. Just before serving, top lasagna with Roasted Red Bell Pepper Dressing (see recipe page 41).

NOTE: You may use either salad shrimp or large shrimp. Large shrimp needs to be cut before layering. Also, be sure to season the vegetables and fish with salt and pepper as you go.

Serves 14

End of the Year Moose Ribs

15 pounds meaty moose ribs

1/2 cup cornstarch

1 cup red wine vinegar

1 cup soy sauce

1 cup brown sugar

1 medium yellow onion, chopped

4 ounces tomato paste

2 tablespoons hot chili sauce

3 ounces sesame oil

2 tablespoons chopped garlic

1 tablespoon grated fresh ginger

Put ribs in a 3-gallon pot and fill with water until the ribs are just submerged. Bring to a boil and simmer for about 1 hour. The meat should be quite tender, but not falling off the bone. While simmering, set aside cornstarch and place all remaining ingredients in a medium sauce pot. Stir together over medium heat. When the moose is ready, add the sauce to the water and cover. Cook for 1/2 hour, and then cool. Once cool, skim off the fat and discard. Pour the remaining liquid into the medium sauce pot and cook over medium heat. Once hot, whisk in cornstarch and simmer until thick. Stir frequently.

Preheat oven to 450°F.

Spread the ribs over a large baking pan and cover with the thickened sauce. Bake until browned. It should take 10 to 20 minutes. Watch closely as overcooking will result in very dry ribs. This should yield about 5 pounds of meat.

Serves 24 to 30

Clay Duck

2 cups cooked rice

1/2 yellow onion, chopped

1 carrot, sliced lengthwise

5 garlic cloves

1 sprig fresh rosemary

Salt and pepper to taste

1/2 cup fresh parsley

1 high-quality duckling

Mix together rice, veggies, and spices. Stuff duck with mixture and sew shut. Brown or wild rice is recommended.

TO COVER THE DUCK

1 teaspoon salt

1 teaspoon pepper

3 tablespoons olive oil

Alder or Hawaiian tea leaves

Parchment paper

18–by–18 inch slab of clay

Preheat oven to 350°F.

Rub the outside of the duck with salt, pepper, and oil. Cover with leaves and wrap tightly with parchment. Tie closed.

For the clay, any type of stoneware is fine, including recycled materials. It should be workable and rolled thin. Place the packaged duck onto one side of the clay slab and fold the other half over it. Seal tightly. At this time, the casing can be decorated with imprints. Bake for 3^1/$_2$ hours. The clay should be hardened, so break gently. Serve with your choice of accompaniments.

NOTE: This is a wonderfully festive dish, often exciting the whole table as the clay is broken into and the feast is revealed. Though preparation is longer, the rewards are great. We once served these as the entrée at one of our much-anticipated annual pirate parties.

Serves 4 to 6

Halibut Cove Style

There is a unique lifestyle in Halibut Cove; it's all about boats, board-walks, and living the art. This artists' studio now shelters three generations of a Halibut Cove family.

SIDE DISHES

Sesame Slaw

A light alternative to the traditional mayonnaise-based coleslaw.

1/4 cup sesame oil

1 tablespoon rice wine vinegar

1 teaspoon honey

1/2 teaspoon roasted chili paste

2 cups thinly sliced green cabbage

2 cups thinly sliced red cabbage

2 carrots, shredded

2 scallions, chopped

1 tablespoon sesame seeds

In a blender, combine sesame oil, vinegar, honey, and chili paste. In large bowl, toss vinaigrette with cabbage, carrots, scallions, and sesame seeds.

Serves 12

Sautéed Kale

3 cloves garlic, minced

1 chili pepper, whole

1 tablespoon olive oil

1 pound kale, de-stemmed and cut into bite-sized pieces

Pinch of salt

In a skillet over medium-low heat, sauté garlic and chili pepper in oil until garlic is browned. Add kale and salt and cook until kale is just wilted.

Serves 4 to 6

Grilled Vegetables

2 zucchini, sliced

1 summer squash

2 carrots, peeled

2 large tomatoes

1 orange pepper, seeded

3 tablespoons olive oil

Salt and pepper to taste

1 small lemon, quartered

Prepare the grill. Slice zucchini, squash, and carrots lengthwise 1/3 inch thick. Quarter tomatoes and pepper. Toss vegetables in a large bowl with olive oil, salt, and pepper. Grill until pepper skin is charred and carrot and squash are softened. Squeeze lemon over vegetables just before serving.

NOTE: This recipe will work for most vegetables. Saltry favorites include asparagus, rings of red onion, and cremini mushrooms.

Serves 12

Kachemak Bay Homestead

Summer is coming to an end, and the last of the salmon are running in the bay. Cows watch from their outposts along the beach. The homesteader's cabin is surrounded by abundant resources and striking wild beauty. A few miles away, an immense river delta has deposited the soil that grows rich salt grass upon which the cattle are fattened for the winter to come. Coal washed from the inland seams provides an endless supply of fuel for heating and cooking, and is gathered from the terra-cotta beach. Decades before the homesteader's cabin stood here with its wooden fences, hay meadows, and garden, the burning coal seams turned the gray clay to a brick red.

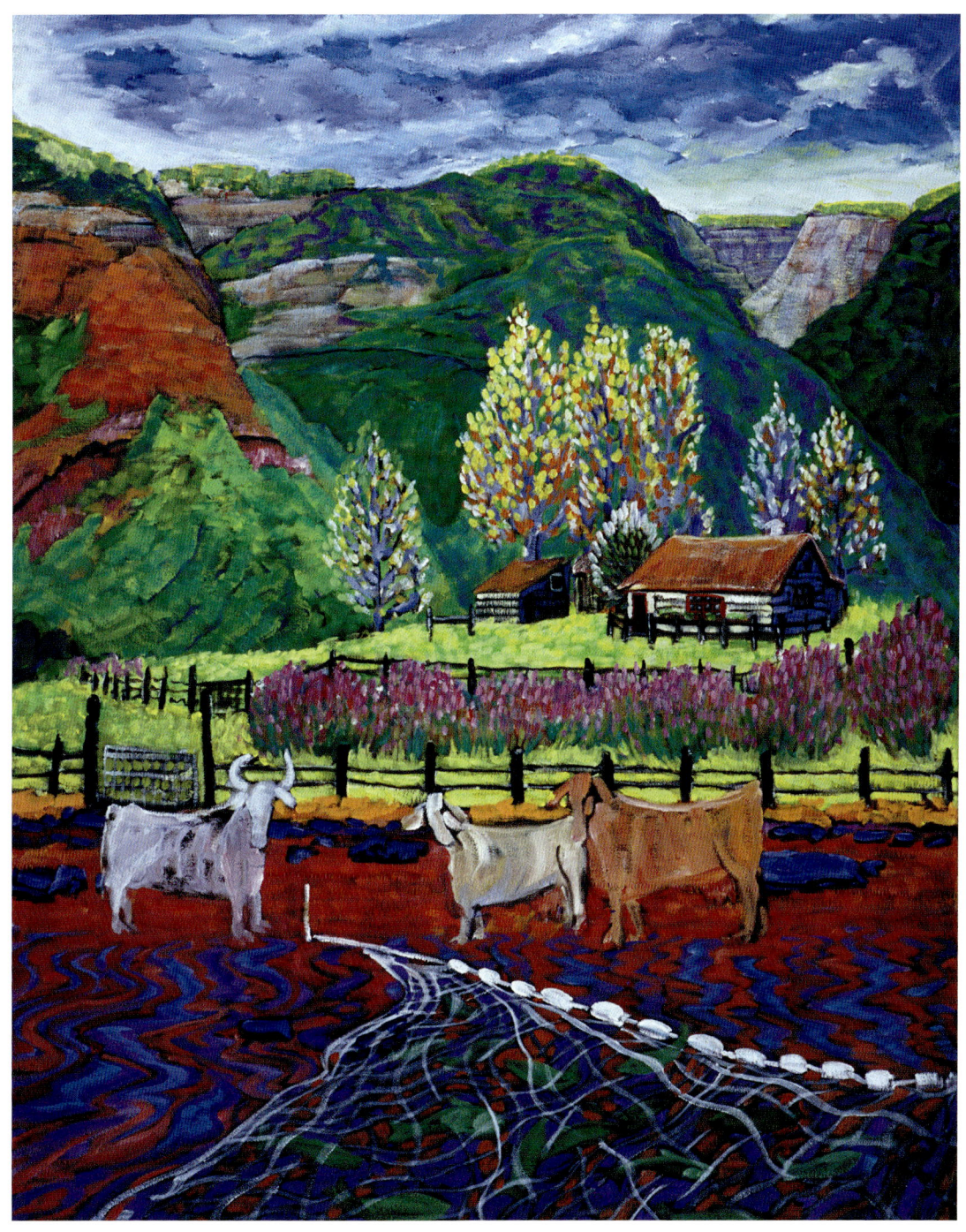

Syd's Holualoa Coconut Rice

1/2 cup shredded sweet coconut

1 cup chopped onion

2 teaspoons finely minced jalapeño
  (3 teaspoons if you prefer spicy)

3 teaspoons minced fresh ginger

1 tablespoon olive oil

2 cups white rice

2 teaspoons salt

31/2 cups unsweetened coconut milk,
  mixed with 1 cup water

3 tablespoons fresh lime juice

4 tablespoons chopped fresh cilantro

Toast shredded coconut in a small skillet over low heat, stirring frequently until golden brown. Set aside to cool. Combine onion, jalapeños, ginger, and oil in heavy saucepan over medium heat, stirring frequently until onion is brown. Add rice and cook for 2 more minutes, stirring constantly. Mix 2 cups of coconut milk with water and salt. Add to pan and bring to boil. Cover the pan and allow to simmer for 10 minutes. Add remaining coconut milk, lime juice, and cilantro. Cover and simmer for 20 minutes or until rice is tender. Sprinkle toasted coconut on top and serve.

Serves 12

Shiitake Potato Cakes

1 cup dried Shiitake mushrooms

3 medium baking potatoes

Oil for pan

1/4 cup finely chopped onion

1 tablespoon soy sauce

2 scallions, finely chopped

Salt and pepper to taste

2 tablespoons sour cream

Reconstitute mushrooms by soaking them in water for about 2 to 3 hours. Drain. Bake potatoes at 400°F for 40 minutes, or until they can be pierced easily by a fork. In a skillet sauté onion and mushrooms with soy sauce until onion is transparent and mushrooms are tender. Combine all ingredients and mix well. Shape into 4 patties, sauté in oil until warm through and golden brown on both sides.

Serves 8

Garlic Mashed Potatoes

1 medium bulb garlic

6 medium russet potatoes,
    peeled and cut into quarters

1/2 cup milk or cream

5 tablespoons butter

2 teaspoons plus pinch of salt, divided

Pepper

Slice top off of garlic bulb, and place bulb in aluminum foil with a bit of olive oil, salt, and pepper. Place foil-wrapped package into 375°F oven for about 30 minutes, or until garlic is soft. Wait until garlic is cool enough to handle, then squeeze garlic paste from cut-off end, much as you would toothpaste from a tube. Bring water to a boil in large pot. Add generous pinch of salt. Add potatoes and cook until tender but still firm, about 15 minutes, then drain. In a small saucepan, heat milk or cream until warm but not boiling. Stir butter into milk, 1 tablespoon at a time. Add garlic and use a fork or wire whisk to blend well. Mash potatoes and half of milk mixture, 2 teaspoons salt, and pepper. Slowly add remaining milk, keeping an eye on the consistency. You don't want the potatoes too runny. Add more salt and pepper to taste.

VARIATION: Potatoes may be left unpeeled, but be sure to wash before cooking. For a deliciously unique flavor, try adding Heidi's secret ingredient: 1 to 2 teaspoons of horseradish.

Serves 12

Mushroom Ragout

1/2 cup butter

1/2 pound shiitake mushrooms, sliced

1/2 pound cremini mushrooms, sliced

2 cloves garlic, minced

1 teaspoon fresh thyme leaves

1/2 cup white wine

1 cup stock (chicken or beef)

1 cup heavy cream

1/2 teaspoon salt

1/2 teaspoon ground black pepper

1 tablespoon thinly cut chives

In a large sauté pan, melt butter. Sauté mushrooms over high heat, searing them on each side before stirring. Add the garlic, thyme, and wine. Cook until the pan is almost dry. Add stock and reduce by half. Add cream and cook until the sauce coats a spoon. Remove from heat and add the salt, pepper, and chives.

NOTE: This is a topping we offer for our buffalo rib eye steak. Also goes well with salmon, giving a full and hearty feel.

Makes 4 cups

Goat Cheese and Roasted Garlic Polenta

2 bulbs garlic

2 tablespoons extra-virgin olive oil

Pinch each salt and black pepper

4 cups chicken or vegetable stock

3 cups whole milk

1 cup heavy cream

1 teaspoon kosher salt

1/2 teaspoon ground black pepper

1 1/2 cups coarsely ground polenta

Zest from 1 lemon

Juice from 1/2 lemon

8 ounces goat cheese

1/2 cup chopped mixed herbs
    (complementing what you serve it with)

Preheat oven to 350ºF.

Cut the top 1/2 inch off of the garlic bulbs, drizzle with olive oil, and sprinkle with salt and pepper. Wrap in foil and place in oven. Roast for about an hour, or until the garlic starts to brown. Remove and cool.

In a large saucepan, place stock, milk, heavy cream, kosher salt, and pepper. Bring to a boil. Slowly whisk in the polenta. Simmer, stirring frequently, for about 20 minutes or until polenta is soft and creamy. Mix in roasted garlic and remaining ingredients. You can easily remove the cloves from the bulb by squeezing from the bottom up. Adjust seasoning to taste.

NOTE: This dish can be made ahead of time and reheated. To keep it creamy, you may need to whisk in additional stock, milk, or cream.

Serves 12

Blue Cheese Butter

1/2 cup softened butter

4 ounces blue cheese

1/2 teaspoon ground black pepper

1/2 cup chopped herbs, chives, and parsley

Combine butter, blue cheese, and pepper. Form into a log and coat with herbs. Slice off pieces to serve. May be stored in the freezer for future use.

NOTE: We serve this on our buffalo rib eye steaks, since they are leaner and can handle the addition of some fat!

Serves 12

Braised Fennel and Shiitake Mushrooms

1 fennel bulb, sliced a 1/2 inch thick

8 ounces shiitake mushroom tops

1 bulb garlic, cloves separated and peeled

1 small onion, sliced

1/2 cup white wine

1 cup stock

1 tablespoon fish sauce

1 tablespoon tamari sauce

1/2 teaspoon ground black pepper

2 sprigs fresh thyme

Preheat oven to 350ºF.

Place all ingredients in a medium baking dish and cover loosely with aluminum foil. Bake for 1 1/2 hours. Vegetables should be tender, not mushy. An excellent accompaniment to grilled salmon shark.

Serves 12

Yellow Curry Sauce

1 tablespoon olive oil

1 small yellow onion, diced

1 jalapeño, seeds removed, and diced

1 small bulb of ginger, sliced

3 cloves garlic, minced

3 tablespoons curry powder

1 tablespoon flour

2 cups stock (chicken, fish, or vegetable)

14 ounces coconut milk

1 tomato, diced

1 teaspoon salt

1 tablespoon lime juice

Heat olive oil in a medium sauce pot, and sauté onion, jalapeño, ginger, and garlic. Cook until onion is translucent, but do not brown. Add curry powder and flour. Stir over medium heat until curry powder is very fragrant. It should take about a minute.

Slowly add stock, stirring constantly to prevent lumps. Add coconut milk, tomato, and salt. Simmer for 20 minutes, stirring occasionally. Remove ginger slices and add lime juice.

MENU SUGGESTION: Serve over salmon, with brown rice and sautéed vegetables.

Serves 12

Waiting for Snow

At the start of September, the impossibly long days of light have begun to wane. Summer inhabitants leave and the ferry ceases its run. The sun is thin, the crows are quiet, and the island turns in on itself, preparing for the darkening days of winter. The old coaling skiff, shored up on the isthmus beach, becomes each year more part of the landscape.

DESSERTS

Swedish Crème

1 cup sugar

2 cups heavy cream

2 cups sour cream

2 teaspoons gelatin

2 teaspoons vanilla

3 tablespoons Frangelico (optional)

2 cups berries (optional)

1 cup chocolate, melted (optional)

Combine sugar, cream, gelatin, and vanilla in a double boiler and cook until sugar is dissolved—about 10 minutes. Prepare wine glasses by putting fruit on the bottom or line the glasses with melted chocolate. Pour the cream mixture on top and drizzle with Frangelico if desired. Refrigerate for at least 2 hours to set crème.

Serves 12

Crème Brûlée

10 large egg yolks
1¼ cups granulated sugar, divided
4 cups heavy cream
Seeds from 2 vanilla beans, split and scraped

Vigorously whisk egg yolks with 1 cup of the granulated sugar in a large bowl, until mixture becomes light in color and sugar has dissolved; set aside. In a medium-sized saucepan, combine heavy cream with vanilla seeds. Heat slowly, stirring constantly to avoid skin forming—do not boil. Slowly pour the cream into the egg mixture, whisking gently. Fill 8 ramekins 3/4 full and place in a baking pan. Pour hot water into baking pan so water level reaches halfway up the sides of the ramekins. Tightly cover pan with a sheet of aluminum foil.

Cook about 45 minutes or until only the very center of the custard appears jelly-like. Remove ramekins from oven and chill for several hours to set custard. Just before serving, put a thin, even layer of the remaining sugar over top of custard and heat with a blowtorch, moving from the edge toward the center.

NOTE: It's also possible to caramelize the sugar under a broiler.

Serves 12

Rowboats

How oars are stowed in or beside the rowboat can be an indication of the owners' habits. In this case they are in a hurry, heading to a cove-style dinner party with lots of fish, shellfish, moose, bear, great bread, big salads, mega desserts, not to mention the homebrew and wine. No cook wants their dish to go unnoticed and no diner wants to miss out on some fabulous flavor. The bachelors are anticipating the food from all the different kitchens with different styles.

Chocolate Cheesecake

A Saltry classic.

  2 cups graham cracker crumbs

  2 1/2 cups sugar, divided

  1/4 cup butter, melted

  3 pounds cream cheese, softened

  6 eggs

  2 cups sour cream

  1 pound high-quality semisweet chocolate

Preheat oven to 250°F.

Prepare a 12-inch springform pan by cutting baking paper in a circle to fit the bottom. Mix graham crackers, 1/2 cup sugar, and butter together and press against bottom and sides of pan, keeping the top edge uniform so it will be attractive when sliced.

Using an electric mixer, beat the cream cheese and sugar together until smooth. Add eggs, 2 at a time, and sour cream, mixing all the while. Melt the chocolate in a double boiler, and when it's completely melted and silky in texture, add it slowly to the cream cheese mixture, beating constantly. Pour into the pan and bake for about 1 1/2 hours. Watch it carefully; you don't want it to crack or the edges to puff up too much. Serve with a drizzle of chocolate and whipped cream.

Serves 24

Peanut Butter Pie

OREO CRUST

2 cups Oreo cookie crumbles

1/2 cup unsalted butter, melted

Using a food processor, grind cookie crumbles until they are fairly uniform in size. Add melted butter and mix until crumbles hold together. Pat into pie pan and be sure to form a lip about a 1/2 inch tall. This will help to contain the ganache topping as you spread it.

FILLING

12 ounces cream cheese

1 1/2 cups peanut butter

1 cup sugar

1 cup heavy cream

Bring cream cheese to room temperature. Once softened, mix together with peanut butter and sugar in a medium-sized bowl. Whip heavy cream until just firm and fold into mixture. Put in crust and let sit while preparing ganache.

GANACHE TOPPING

2 ounces bittersweet chocolate

1/2 cup heavy cream

Melt the chocolate in a double boiler and stir in heavy cream until mixed. Pour over pie filling, using a spatula to spread it evenly over the surface.

NOTE: This pie requires no baking and can be easily frozen to serve at a later date. Best served cold.

Serves 12

Alana's Kodiak Explosion Cake

3 cups flour

1/2 cup unsweetened cocoa powder

2 teaspoons baking soda

2 cups sugar

1 teaspoon salt

2 cups water

1/2 cup vegetable oil

2 tablespoons white vinegar

2 teaspoons vanilla extract

MIDDLE LAYER

2 cans sweetened condensed milk,
   for caramel sauce

1 1/2 cups chopped roasted nuts

1 cup chopped bittersweet chocolate

CARAMEL SAUCE

Fill a medium-sized pot with water and put on to boil. Remove the labels from the cans of sweetened condensed milk and put the unopened cans into the pot. Do not leave unattended and monitor water level; do not let water evaporate to expose the cans. Once it begins to boil, time for 1 hour and 15 minutes. Remove cans and set aside. Open cans while warm but do so with caution. Pours best if added to a small bowl and stirred. May be reheated if too stiff to pour.

Preheat oven to 350°F.

Grease a 9-by-13-inch baking pan.

Sift together flour, cocoa, and baking soda into a large bowl. Add sugar and salt, then water, oil, vinegar, and vanilla. Whisk thoroughly until all ingredients are well blended. Put 3 cups of batter into the greased pan. Use a spatula to spread evenly. Bake for about 15 minutes. The batter should be cooked, not gooey. Remove from oven and evenly sprinkle nuts and chocolate chunks over warm cake. Then add caramel evenly over the top. Cover with remaining batter and return to oven. Bake for an additional 35 minutes, or until cake is set. Should be moist, but again, not gooey. Let cool and serve directly from the pan.

NOTE: This is a favorite among the kitchen crew. It is so enjoyed that we only allow ourselves to bake it in intervals for fear of expanding waistlines!

Serves 24

Fig and Pecan Bread Pudding

8 eggs

2¼ cups granulated sugar

Pinch salt

1 teaspoon vanilla extract

3 cups whole milk

1 cup heavy cream

½ cup bourbon or dark rum (optional)

8 ounces dried figs, chopped in halves or quarters

1 cup chopped pecans

6 cups stale bread, cut into ½-inch cubes
    (we prefer Saltry Bread, of course!)

⅛ cup unsalted butter

Preheat oven to 350°F.

In a large mixing bowl whisk together eggs, 2 cups of the sugar, salt, and vanilla extract. Whisk in milk, heavy cream, and bourbon or rum. Add figs, pecans, and bread, mixing to evenly distribute. Let soak for 30 minutes.

In a 9-by-9-inch baking dish, melt the butter in the oven. Pour in bread mixture. Sprinkle remaining ¼ cup of sugar over the top. Bake for 1 hour, checking after 45 minutes. The top should be browning and the center should be fully set.

Serve warm with Caramel Sauce (see recipe page 93) and whipped cream.

TIP: The bread pudding will set and be easier to cut if you bake ahead of time and chill in the refrigerator overnight. This is one of the few dishes that reheats well in a microwave. But it is also delicious hot out of the oven!

Serves 12

Warm Soft Chocolate Cakes

4 ounces bittersweet chocolate

1/2 cup unsalted butter

2 eggs

2 egg yolks

1/2 cup sugar

2 teaspoons flour
   (plus flour for dusting the molds)

This recipe yields 4 to 6 individual cakes to be baked in 8-ounce metal cake molds. Prepare the molds by covering with a generous layer of butter and then lightly dusting with flour.

Melt the chocolate and butter together using a double boiler. While waiting, use a whisk to beat the eggs, yolks, and sugar until thick. Once melted, stir the 2 mixtures together and quickly add the flour. Pour into the molds. Store in the refrigerator until ready to bake. When the time comes, preheat the oven to 425°F and bake for 7 to 9 minutes.

NOTE: These cakes are served hot and should be molten in the center if properly cooked. When done, the edges of the cakes should be raised with a slight depression in the center.

Serves 6

Toby Tyler's Rosehip Pie

3/4 cup sugar

1/2 cup Bisquick

2 tablespoons butter

1 (13-ounce) can evaporated milk

2 eggs

16 ounces thawed rosehip puree

2 1/2 teaspoons pumpkin pie spice

2 teaspoons vanilla

1/4 teaspoon nutmeg

Preheat oven to 350°F.

Grease a 10-inch pie tin. Mix all ingredients in a blender until smooth. Pour into prepared pie tin and sprinkle with nutmeg. Bake for 45 to 55 minutes, rotating the pie once about halfway through.

ROSEHIP PUREE

Pick many rosehips, at least a gallon-bucket full. Remove any stems and the dead sepals. Cover with water in a large pot and bring to a boil. Simmer and add more water as needed. Press resulting mass through a conical aluminum mortar or sieve with a wooden pestle. This is easiest when the mixture is not too thick and still hot. (Take heart, this is by far the most difficult part of the process.) Be vigilant in extracting the rock-hard seeds; they could break a tooth. Either use puree immediately or freeze for later.

Serves 8

Rosehips

As summer fades into fall, rose petals disappear. Beautiful rosehips replace the blossoms, each one unique when examined closely as in this painting. In early days, when very little fruit was available in Alaska, creative cooks made rosehips into jams, pies, cakes, and teas. Rosehips are high in vitamin C.

Toni's Cove-Style Apple Pie

6 cups tart apples, peeled, cored, and sliced
   (approximately 5 Granny Smith apples)

1 cup brown sugar

1 tablespoon cinnamon

1 tablespoon lemon juice

1 teaspoon lemon zest

1/4 teaspoon vanilla

Preheat oven to 425°F.

Mix all ingredients together in a medium-sized bowl and let sit while preparing crust. Lightly grease pie pan with shortening. Line with bottom crust. Fill with apple filling, dribbling any remaining juice over apples. Cover with top crust, crimp edges, and prick the top with fork. Bake for 20 minutes, reduce heat to 350°F, and bake another 30 to 35 minutes until crust is golden brown. Let cool and serve with vanilla ice cream or a slice of Cheddar cheese.

GRANDMA'S PIECRUST

1 cup flour

7 tablespoons vegetable shortening

1 tablespoon cornstarch

1/2 teaspoon salt

1/4 cup cold milk

Whisk together flour, cornstarch, and salt. Add shortening and mix with a fork until shortening is coated with flour mixture forming small flaky pieces. Add milk a little at a time while continuing to mix gently. Pick up dough carefully with floured hands and form into a ball. Divide in half. Roll each ball out on a floured surface.

Serves 8

Mom's Rhubarb Custard Pie

4 eggs

1 cup sugar

3/4 cup brown sugar

1/8 teaspoon salt

1/8 teaspoon nutmeg

1/4 teaspoon ginger

1/4 teaspoon cinnamon

4 cups 1/2-inch pieces of rhubarb

1 tablespoon lemon juice

2 tablespoons butter

1 Grandma's Piecrust

Preheat oven to 350°F.

Whip eggs with sugar, salt, and spices. Put rhubarb into piecrust, then sprinkle with lemon juice. Pour whipped egg mixture over rhubarb and place thin slices of butter around the top. Cover with top crust, crimp edges, and make 6 slashes with the tip of a knife. Bake for about 50 minutes.

Serves 8

The Homer Hill

The rolling hills of Homer are displaying the last weeks of the short Alaskan summer. Abundant plant life has grown furiously under the sun of the long summer days, but is now nipped by frost, which makes the colors rich and vibrant. Cool air swirls with fireweed fluff and mingles with the aromas of cranberry and cottonwood. The Kenai Mountains are barely visible above the towering vegetation that will soon be bent downward by the snow. Summer rushes into fall and the inevitable darkness of winter.

SMOKING & SALTING FISH

Smoking Fish

Smoked fish makes a wonderful accent to any dish, or is a terrific appetizer or snack on its own. There are a number of home smokers available; the price varies widely as does the capacity. Experiment with the type of chips you use from the wide variety available. At the Saltry we usually use cherry or alder chips.

It is possible to smoke any type of fish, though not all of them hold smoked flavor well. At the Saltry we regularly use smoked salmon and smoked black cod, and have tried (and enjoyed) smoked shark. On the following page are two standard marinades that always work well and always taste good. Both work well for the recipes requiring smoked fish listed earlier in this book.

Smoking Marinade

4 pounds salmon or other fish, cut into
   1-inch-wide boneless strips

4 cups soy sauce

1/2 cup sesame oil

1 1/2 cups brown sugar

1 cup honey

2 tablespoons grated ginger

6 cloves garlic, minced

1 tablespoon chili paste

Mix up marinade and soak fish for 24 hours.

NOTE: This recipe is for 4 pounds of fish, but tailor the ingredients to suit your tastes and the amount of fish you have.

Makes 2 quarts

Candied Salmon

1 cup soy sauce

1/2 onion, sliced

2 cloves garlic, peeled

2-inch cube of fresh ginger, skinned

1 cup brown sugar

4 pounds salmon, cut into
   1-inch-wide boneless strips

Combine soy sauce, onion, garlic, and ginger in a blender. Form a paste by mixing the liquid with brown sugar. Slather the fish with paste and refrigerate for 3 days or until fish strips are stiff. Smoke according to smokehouse directions. If you are using it to make the Saltry's Salmon Pâté (see recipe page 14), smoke an hour longer than suggested.

Serves 12

Salting Fish

This is the way we salt the fish used to make pickled salmon and poke. You can also smoke salted fish. These are general guidelines; measurements vary depending on the amount of fish you want to salt, but the system stays the same.

Pour 1/2 inch of fine salt in the bottom of a deep baking dish. Lay fillets skin-side down and cover with 1/4 inch of salt. Layer fillets flesh to flesh and skin to skin, with 1/4 inch of salt between each layer. Cover top layer of fish with 1/4 inch of salt and weigh it down with a glass dish or something similarly heavy. Refrigerate. It usually takes about 2 weeks for salmon to get completely hard, but fish will keep like this for ages.

When you're ready to use the salted fish, remove the bones and cut into cubes (for pickled salmon and poke). Cover with water and soak in several changes of cold water for 8 to 48 hours (depending on taste). Stir the soaking fish occasionally so that the salt soaks out evenly. If you're preparing the fish to use in poke, we recommend using ice water.

Lagoon Fishing

In the shaded and cool estuary, the dominant sound is the rumble of the creek pouring down, over, and through the rocks to meet the sea. Just below the surface, hundreds of king salmon swirl quietly, though clearly visible to the fishermen standing on the edge of their skiffs. The experts sit quietly, watching their bobbers with veteran eyes, while others cast their lures. The thrill of the wait is overwhelming, and each cast of the lure is carefully aimed. The awaited moment arrives and "BAM": the fish is on the line. The silence is now broken by the mad scramble to retrieve their prey.

ACKNOWLEDGMENTS

A special thank you to Alana Branson of Kodiak and Steven Obendorf of Soldotna, both Saltry Partners, for the additions and revisions that helped pave the way for the cookbook's second edition.

Thanks to Tony Stanfill, Candace Branson, Josiah Campbell, Kori Wanner, Toni Maury, Sydney Bishop, Marlene Miller, Donna and Jack Bennett, Susan Glassow, Lucinda Sidelinger, Toby Tyler, Diana Tillion, Diana Conway, Jay Greene, Dan Fowler, and Patricia Green for their contributions of recipes and help with editing.

Also, thanks to my mom, Diana Tillion, who, regrettably, died in 2010, but gave me a lifetime of history, art, and cooking.

A huge thank you to all the talented and creative individuals who have been part of the Saltry crews, past and present, who have, over the years, added their own special touches bringing these recipes to life.

Thanks always to master artist Alex Combs. In the spring of 1979, Alex, art department chair at the University of Alaska Anchorage, retired and moved to Halibut Cove. As a young artist he had first moved to Alaska, and some say he brought modern art with him. Alex loved to teach; he was a master at clay and painting, and in his studio I learned the art of decorating. Alex taught us to outline, drawing the designs forward, and I ultimately took these techniques to painting. Without Alex, I would never have been me.

And finally, I simply must thank my husband, Dave. Years ago, I enjoyed putting on flamboyant dinner parties, which with his encouragement, became a fine art restaurant, featuring local art and tables set with healthy food from the sea. The Saltry and this cookbook are testaments to a great partnership.

Island Ponies

Marian had her first horse when she was five. It was made of wood—the natural knee of a spruce tree, with one gray eye and one brown, a nylon mane and painted a ferocious shade of red. She thinks it set a precedent for a life of red ponies. She got her first real horse at twelve, and her grandpa fished in her stead so she could spend the summer riding and training it.

ABOUT THE ARTIST

Marian believes that her art is inextricably linked with her environment—that the two things can not be separated. She draws inspiration from living in Halibut Cove. Working on fishing boats, riding horses, and island life are all recurrent themes in her paintings. Marian explains art as an expression of the sensuality of life—a catalyst for evoking smells and emotions. She believes that life itself is art, an organic sculpture shifting within the different frames of the artist's perceptions.

Marian Tillion was born in 1953 in Seldovia, Alaska. Her parents, Clem and Diana, had recently settled in Halibut Cove, and Marian was the first child born into the ghost town that remained after the collapse of the herring fishery. Much of her childhood was spent on the water. She started fishing with her father when she was ten—after proving she was strong enough by picking him up. Horses have always been a ruling passion in Marian's life. Her first horse was brought to the island on a barge when she was twelve.

Marian attended college at Cal Poly University in San Luis Obispo, California, earning a degree in animal science. To pay for college she obtained her 100-ton marine license in 1974 and began skippering commercial boats.

While at Cal Poly University, Marian also studied art and later attended the Art Students League in New York City. Further art education included studies in clay with potters Al Tennant, Mark Ervice, and Alex Combs, and classes and workshops in watercolor, silk screen, monotypes, batik, and painting from life. Marian received her first Juror's Choice Award for an opaque watercolor accepted into the 1985 juried art show at the Pratt Museum in Homer. Since that first award in 1985 she has received many Juror's Choice Awards and Honorable Mentions, as well as several State and Museum purchase awards. Her first solo exhibition of size was at the Pratt Museum in 1990. Although in recent years Marian has concentrated on painting, she has also created clay sculpture and wearable art, and each year decorates 90 to 100 platters for her restaurant.

When Marian and her husband, Dave Beck, built the Saltry in 1984, it provided another avenue for artistic expression. Marian considers the Saltry a piece of functioning art—smooth against rough, exquisite dining against a rugged backdrop. The building itself is an artistic structure, housing handmade plates, mosaic tables, and creatively presented food.

INDEX

Alana's Kodiak Explosion Cake,
  92–93
Apple Pie, Toni's Cove-Style, 98

bacon
  Halibut with Hot Bacon
    Dressing, 48
  Rhubarb and Bacon
    Vinaigrette, 42
basil
  Marian's Buffalo Lasagna,
    65–66
  Pesto Halibut, 46
  Sweet Basil Dressing, 41
bell peppers
  Roasted Red Bell Pepper
    Dressing, 41
  Smoked Salmon Yam Yums,
    55–56
Blue Cheese Butter, 83
Bouillabaisse, Trey's, 35
Braised Fennel and Shiitake
  Mushrooms, 84
Bread, Saltry, 13
Bread Pudding, Fig and Pecan, 94
Buffalo Lasagna, Marian's, 65–66
Buffaloaf, Tony's, 67–68

cabbage
  Sesame Slaw, 75
cakes, sweet
  Alana's Kodiak Explosion
    Cake, 92–93
  Warm Soft Chocolate Cakes,
    95
cakes and patties, savory
  Dave's Salmon Patties, 52
  Halibut Cakes, 48–49
  Shiitake Potato Cakes, 79

Candied Salmon, 102
Ceviche, Halibut, 17
Ceviche, Papaya, 18
cheese
  Blue Cheese Butter, 83
  Goat Cheese and Roasted
    Garlic Polenta, 82–83
  Marian's Buffalo Lasagna,
    65–66
  Smoked Salmon Yam Yums,
    55–56
  Steven's Shrimp and Cod
    Lasagna, 68–70
Cheesecake, Chocolate, 90
chocolate, cocoa
  Alana's Kodiak Explosion
    Cake, 92–93
  Peanut Butter Pie, 91
  Warm Soft Chocolate Cakes,
    95
Chocolate Cheesecake, 90
cilantro
  Halibut Pickled with Citrus,
    17
  Papaya Ceviche, 18
  Papaya Salsa, 62
Cinnamon Shrimp, 25
Cioppino, 36–37
Citrus, Halibut Pickled with,
  17–18
clams
  Cioppino, 36–37
  Coconut Seafood Chowder,
    34
  Sable Fish Chowder, 31–32
  Trey's Bouillabaisse, 35
Clay Duck, 72–73
coconut
  Coconut Seafood Chowder, 34

Syd's Holualoa Coconut Rice,
  78
  Yellow Curry Sauce, 85
Cod Lasagna, Steven's Shrimp
  and, 68–70
crab
  Stuffed China Root Red,
    54–55
cream cheese
  Chocolate Cheesecake, 90
  Peanut Butter Pie, 91
  Salmon Pâté, 14
  Steven's Shrimp and Cod
    Lasagna, 68–70
Crème Brûleé, 88
cucumber
  Refrigerator Pickles, 43
Curry Sauce, Yellow, 85
Custard Pie, Mom's Rhubarb, 99

Dave's Salmon Patties, 52
dill
  Garlic-Dill Aioli, 48–49
  Refrigerator Pickles, 43
dressings, salad
  garlic, oil, and vinegar, 66
  Raspberry Poppy Seed
    Vinaigrette, 40
  Rhubarb and Bacon
    Vinaigrette, 42
  Roasted Red Bell Pepper
    Dressing, 41
  Sweet Basil Dressing, 41
Duck, Clay, 72–73

End of the Year Moose Ribs, 71

Fennel and Shiitake Mushrooms,
  Braised, 84

Fig and Pecan Bread Pudding, 94
Fish Stock, 32
Garlic Mashed Potatoes, 80
Garlic Polenta, Roasted, and
    Goat Cheese, 82–83
Garlic-Dill Aioli, 48–49
Ginger Salmon, with Sesame, 51
Goat Cheese and Roasted Garlic
    Polenta, 82–83
Grilled Halibut, 45
Grilled Salmon with Raspberry
    Sauce, 51
Grilled Vegetables, 76

halibut
    Cioppino, 36–37
    Coconut Seafood Chowder, 34
    Grilled Halibut, 45
    Halibut Cakes, 48–49
    Halibut Pickled with Citrus,
        17–18
    Halibut with Hot Bacon
        Dressing, 48
    Papaya Ceviche, 18
    Paprika Soy Halibut, 45
    Pesto Halibut, 46
heavy cream
    Crème Brûleé, 88
    Fig and Pecan Bread Pudding,
        94
    Peanut Butter Pie, 91
    Swedish Crème, 87
Hot Bacon Dressing, 48

Kachemak Bay Blue Mussels, 28
Kale, Sautéed, 75
Korean Poke, Walter's, 22
Korean Shark, Spicy, 61

Lucinda's Baked Oysters, 27

Marian's Buffalo Lasagna,
    65–66

Mom's Rhubarb Custard Pie, 99
Moose Ribs, End of the Year, 71
mushrooms
    Braised Fennel and Shiitake
        Mushrooms, 84
    Mushroom Ragout, 81
    Shiitake Potato Cakes, 79
mussels
    Cioppino, 36–37
    Kachemak Bay Blue Mussels,
        28
    Trey's Bouillabaisse, 35

Nori Rolls, Vegetable, 24
nuts
    Alana's Kodiak Explosion
        Cake, 92–93
    Fig and Pecan Bread Pudding,
        94
    Peanut Butter Pie, 91

Oysters, Lucinda's Baked, 27

Papaya Ceviche, 18
Papaya Salsa, 62
Paprika Soy Halibut, 45
pasta
    Marian's Buffalo Lasagna,
        65–66
    Smoked Salmon Pasta, 58
    Steven's Shrimp and Cod
        Lasagna, 68–70
Pâté, Salmon, 14
Peanut Butter Pie, 91
Pesto Halibut, 46
Pickled Halibut with Citrus,
    17–18
Pickled Salmon, 15
pie, savory
    Shark Pie, 63
pie, sweet
    Mom's Rhubarb Custard Pie,
        99

Peanut Butter Pie, 91
    Toby Tyler's Rosehip Pie, 96
    Toni's Cove-Style Apple Pie,
        98
piecrust
    Grandma's Piecrust, 98–99
    Oreo Crust, 91
Poke, Original Saltry, 21
Poke, Walter's Korean, 22
Polenta, Goat Cheese and
    Roasted Garlic, 82–83
poppy seeds
    Raspberry Poppy Seed
        Vinaigrette, 40
potato
    Garlic Mashed Potatoes, 80
    Shiitake Potato Cakes, 79

Raspberry Poppy Seed
    Vinaigrette, 40
Raspberry Sauce, 51
Refrigerator Pickles, 43
Rhubarb and Bacon Vinaigrette,
    42
Rhubarb Custard Pie, Mom's, 99
rice
    Clay Duck, 72–73
    Stuffed China Poot Red,
        54–55
    Syd's Holualoa Coconut Rice,
        78
    Vegetable Nori Rolls, 24–25
Roasted Red Bell Pepper
    Dressing, 41
Rosehip Pie, Toby Tyler's, 96

Sable Fish Chowder, 31–32
salad, green
    romaine, feta, and kalamata,
        66
    Vibrant Volcano Salad, 39–40
salmon
    Candied Salmon, 102

Coconut Seafood Chowder, 34
Dave's Salmon Patties, 52
Grilled Salmon with Raspberry Sauce, 51
Halibut (or Salmon) Cakes, 48–49
Pickled Salmon, 15
Salmon Pâté, 14
Sesame Ginger Salmon, 51
Smoked Salmon Pasta, 58
Smoked Salmon Yam Yums, 55–56
Stuffed China Poot Red, 54–55
salt, rock
　Lucinda's Baked Oysters, 27
salted fish
　how to, 103
　Pickled Salmon, 15
Saltry Bread, 13
Saltry Poke, Original, 21
Saltry Summer Soup, 37
Sautéed Kale, 75
seafood of choice
　Original Saltry Poke, 21
　Smoking Marinade, 102
　Trey's Bouillabaisse, 35
　Walter's Korean Poke, 22
seaweed
　Walter's Korean Poke, 22
Sesame Ginger Salmon, 51
Sesame Slaw, 75
Shark, Spicy Korean, 61
Shark Pie, 63
Shiitake Potato Cakes, 79
shrimp
　Cinnamon Shrimp, 25
　Steven's Shrimp and Cod Lasagna, 68–70
　Trey's Bouillabaisse, 35
smoked fish
　how to, 101

Sable Fish Chowder, 31–32
Salmon Pâté, 14
Smoked Salmon Pasta, 58
Smoked Salmon Yam Yums, 55–56
Smoking Marinade, 102
sour cream
　Chocolate Cheesecake, 90
　Marian's Buffalo Lasagna, 65–66
　Salmon Pâté, 14
　Swedish Crème, 87
Soy Halibut, Paprika, 45
Spicy Korean Shark, 61
Steven's Shrimp and Cod Lasagna, 68–70
stock
　Braised Fennel and Shiitake Mushrooms, 84
　Goat Cheese and Roasted Garlic Polenta, 82–83
　Mushroom Ragout, 81
　Sable Fish Chowder, 31
　Saltry Summer Soup, 37
　Steven's Shrimp and Cod Lasagna, 68–70
　Trey's Bouillabaisse, 35
　Yellow Curry Sauce, 85
Stuffed China Poot Red, 54–55
Swedish Crème, 87
Sweet Basil Dressing, 41
Syd's Holualoa Coconut Rice, 78

Toby Tyler's Rosehip Pie, 96
Toni's Cove-Style Apple Pie, 98
Tony's Buffaloaf, 67–68
toppings and dressings, savory
　Blue Cheese Butter, 83
　Garlic-Dill Aioli, 48
　Hot Bacon Dressing, 48
　Mushroom Ragout, 81
　Papaya Salsa, 62

Raspberry Sauce, 51
Smoking Marinade, 102
Yellow Curry Sauce, 85
toppings and dressings, sweet
　Caramel Sauce, 93
Trey's Bouillabaisse, 35

vanilla
　Crème Brûleé, 88
　Swedish Crème, 87
vegetable dishes
　Braised Fennel and Shiitake Mushrooms, 84
　Grilled Vegetables, 76
　Refrigerator Pickles, 43
　Sautéed Kale, 75
　Sesame Slaw, 75
　Vegetable Nori Rolls, 24–25
Vibrant Volcano Salad, 39–40

Walter's Korean Poke, 22
Warm Soft Chocolate Cakes, 95
wine and spirits
　Braised Fennel and Shiitake Mushrooms, 84
　Cioppino, 36–37
　Fig and Pecan Bread Pudding, 94
　Fish Stock, 32
　Kachemak Bay Blue Mussels, 28
　Mushroom Ragout, 81
　Sable Fish Chowder, 31–32
　Smoked Salmon Pasta, 58
　Steven's Shrimp and Cod Lasagna, 68–70
　Stuffed China Poot Red, 54–55
　Swedish Crème, 87

Yam Yums, Smoked Salmon, 55–56
Yellow Curry Sauce, 85

An Adventure

By October, the Grewingk Glacier River is a dry bed because the glacial lake has begun to freeze. On a rare occasion, the weather is calm enough to load the horses on a barge and head for Glacier Spit. After a five-mile ride up the moraine, across the dry river bed, and around the lake, riders can behold the awesomeness of the glacier. A glorious yet risky undertaking, there is no lingering to visit the sole resident. If the weather turns foul and the horses cannot be loaded for a safe return to their own island, they could be stormbound for weeks.